You'll love this book as much as you hate your job.

45 cards for decorating your cubicle, insulting coworkers, and justifying your excessive drinking.

Brook Lundy and Duncan Mitchell

STERLING
New York

STERLING
New York

An Imprint of Sterling Publishing
387 Park Avenue South
New York, NY 10016

4 6 8 10 9 7 5 3

© 2011 by someecards, Inc.
www.someecards.com

Distributed in Canada by Sterling Publishing
c/o Canadian Manda Group, 165 Dufferin Street Toronto, Ontario, Canada M6K 3H6
Distributed in the United Kingdom by GMC Distribution Services
Castle Place, 166 High Street, Lewes, East Sussex, England BN7 1XU
Distributed in Australia by Capricorn Link (Australia) Pty. Ltd.
P.O. Box 704, Windsor, NSW 2756, Australia

Sterling ISBN 978-1-4027-8050-9

For information about custom editions, special sales, premium and corporate purchases, please contact
Sterling Special SalesDepartment at 800-805-5489 or specialsales@sterlingpublishing.com.

Introduction

Are you running out of ways to waste valuable business hours? Then you're going to love the someecards workplace book! This best-of collection is from the subversive, hilarious, and barely employable minds at someecards.com. That means you'll have 45 witty and obnoxious tear-out postcards for communicating with underlings, bosses, new employees, hungover co-workers, and the wide array of people you've sexually harassed throughout your career.

Think of all the time you'll save by not having to send or respond to passive-aggressive emails! And instead of just trying to look busy all day, now you can genuinely appear diligent by walking around the office, aimlessly handing out cards. In just minutes you can turn down a pointless meeting request, complain about a new project, then go ask for a raise! Finally, you can say exactly what you feel until security escorts you out of the building.

Too lazy to walk ten feet to hand someone a card? Then consider this book the perfect ornament for your office, cubicle, or other inhumane desk space. And don't forget, small gifts are a great way to kiss ass. A recent workplace study* showed that 98% of promotions and raises are directly tied to the number of someecards books purchased for superiors. So if you want to be a billionaire CEO, it all starts with buying hundreds of copies of this book!

*totally buy this book

We're concerned your job is interfering with your drinking.

someecards

someecards

som**ee**cards

I've stopped even pretending to do anything around here.

som**ee**cards

som**ee**cards

You've been distant since the sexual harassment.

someecards

som**ee**cards

We're willing to do whatever it takes to keep you in this dead-end job.

som**ee**cards

Sorry I called, emailed, or IM'd you from three feet away.

som**ee**cards

I need a time billing code
for not doing shit.

som**ee**cards

Please stop
scheduling
Friday afternoon
meetings.

som**ee**cards

I couldn't get through Mondays without knowing you're equally miserable.

someecards

Let's spend countless hours preparing for a meeting that will be delayed, canceled, or misrepresented.

som**ee**cards

We need to discuss the impact you're having on the men's bathroom.

someecards

som**ee**cards

I'll be in late because I'm hungover or have a job interview.

som**ee**cards

som**ee**cards

Let's discuss my
freelance rate.

someecards

I deserve a raise for doing a half-assed job.

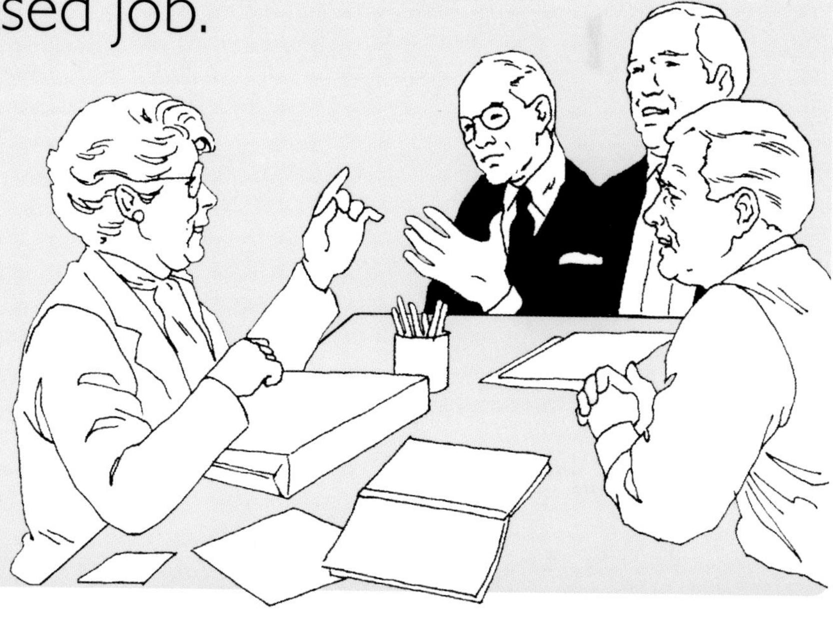

som**ee**cards

I can tell that you've pretended to work very hard on this project.

someecards

I think you misinterpreted the tone of my email.

som**ee**cards

Just getting on your radar because I may need something from you soon.

som**ee**cards

som**ee**cards

Thanks for being a job reference despite what you know.

som**ee**cards

Appearing busy to avoid being laid off has become more exhausting than actually working.

som**ee**cards

Sorry your boss
is an asshole like
everyone else's
on earth.

som**ee**cards

Your cell phone ringtone is damaging your career.

som**ee**cards

someecards

I have a policy of not dating people at work whom I don't find attractive.

someecards

someecards

Sorry I accidentally cc'd you on an email insulting you.

som**ee**cards

som**ee**cards

Never again will your personal water bottle make contact with the communal water cooler spout.

som**ee**cards

Welcome to
the company.

som**ee**cards

I send pointless emails late at night to impress coworkers.

som**ee**cards

I love pretending
I have the courage
to quit my job.

some**ee**cards

I can barely wait to take credit for your great ideas.

someecards

someecards

Your meeting is a high priority if there's free food.

som**ee**cards

Sorry your post-vacation workload has completely negated all the benefits of your vacation.

someecards

I own you.

somee cards

som**ee**cards

I or the company decided it's time for me to leave.

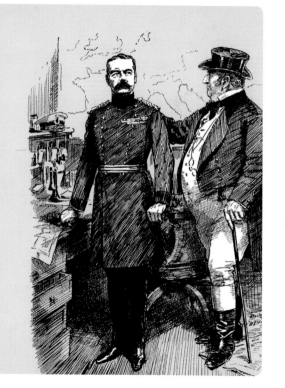

som**ee**cards

I could never replace you because it would be too costly and time-consuming.

someecards

I'm much more efficient at work when I cry at my desk instead of in the bathroom.

som**ee**cards

Author Bios

Brook Lundy is President, Head Writer, and Unpaid Intern of someecards.com. Before cofounding someecards, he was a copywriter in online advertising for over a decade, where his claim to absurd fame was the award-winning ShaveEverywhere.com website. He spent several years writing humor essays for publications such as *Details* and *The New York Times*, as well as writing and performing in a sketch comedy troupe.

Duncan Mitchell was born in New York and raised in San Francisco. He's been a package designer for The Clorox Company, an award-winning creative director in online advertising, and a peanut vendor at Candlestick Park. Currently he lives in New York where he is CEO, Assistant to the CEO, and Art Director at someecards.com.

Contributors: Andrea Bichsel, Heath Bodell, Jon Bogran, Matt Cheplic, Shira Danan, Jesse Darling, Sandy Dietrick, Andrew Kosow, Justin Laub, Lauren Le Vine, Danny Palmer, Eric Schlakman, J. Courtney Sullivan, Jerry Tamburro